FROM

BOYHOOD

TO

REDCAP

Derek Dawes

To Margaret, my lovely wife, for persuading me to write this
x

Chapter 1

DEREK DAWES d.o.b.17th July 1934.

This is an account of events and happenings which occurred during my first twenty-three years, based on memories and recollections.

I hope that whoever reads it will see that a twenty-three-year-old of my generation (born in the early 1930s) would experience things that a modern-day twenty-three-year-old never will.

I was born on 17th July 1934 in the city of Plymouth, Devon. My father was Albert Wyatt Dawes and my mother was Sheila Dawes, nee Hollywood. My father was in the Royal Navy serving on cruisers and my mother worked as a barmaid. We lived at (Rear) 53 Emma Place, Stonehouse, Plymouth. I also had a brother born on 23rd March 1938 called Gordon.

I have some clear memories up to when I was five years old (17th July 1939). When I was three and riding a tricycle I crashed into railings and my bottom teeth went through my bottom lip. I still have a lump on the inside of my lip to this day. My second memory is when I fell out of a tree in our front garden onto railings and was taken to hospital for an operation for a rupture. I remember the nurses were singing a song being played on the radio by Bing Crosby, it was titled '*Don't fence me in*'.

My third memory is starting school at St Georges, Stonehouse, aged five years old and the Second World War starting two weeks later. We were given gas masks at school and told to carry them to school every day. The city started to organise children to leave as evacuees, however, my mother said she would keep me with her so that was it…I never left Plymouth.

The city started to get its defences ready and I remember going to Devils Point, which was a beach area on the edge of Stonehouse. At one end, called Eastern Kings, Royal Marines put up barbed wire and they also set up a machine gun at the other end called Western Kings. A proper anti-aircraft post was built with a searchlight, barrage balloon, and large anti-aircraft guns. The Marines also put an old tank turret at the Devonport end of Halfpenny Bridge to defend it. Drakes Island was fortified and a fort was built in the centre of the breakwater, a couple of big guns from an old battleship were put into the citadel.

At a place called Mount Batton, the RAF kept three Sunderland flying boats and several torpedo boats. Other searchlights and barrage balloons were placed in various parks. One of my uncles arranged for an Anderson shelter to be put into our front garden, but no air raids happened in 1939. However, Plymouth with its naval dockyard, marine barracks, and Millbay docks would be a prime target for the Germans, and living beside it made Stonehouse a danger area.

1940 started quietly, the city tested air raid sirens, which would give us warning of German planes coming. We had our first air raid on 20th March. It was a taste of things to come. The first raids were carried out by just a couple of dozen planes and whilst they caused damage and even killed people they were not enough to stop the city from carrying on as usual.

Sporadic raids came during 1940 and we were beginning to know how to deal with them. I will describe what we did:

When the siren went off I put on my siren suit and shoes and picked up a torch. I got my brother into his suit as well. Then it was my job to take him to the Anderson shelter (whilst my mother was putting tea into a thermos flask). Once at the shelter door I got in first and lit a candle on a small table, then I helped my brother to get in and sat him in the bottom bed of a bunk bed. You had to go down about four feet to get in the shelter. My mother would lock the house up and come to the shelter door, pass down the thermos flask, and always say the same thing before she left, and that was, 'Don't unlock the shelter door unless you hear my voice'.

She would then leave to patrol the local streets as an ARP (which stands for Air Raid Precautions, although they were also known as Air Raid Wardens), while my brother and I were alone in the shelter. I was the man of the house (I was seven).

From Boyhood To Redcap

I can see my mother now, standing outside the shelter dressed in dungarees, wellington boots, and wearing a steel helmet with a stirrup pump in one hand and a bucket of sand in the other. She had to be a brave woman to have walked around during raids whilst we were in a shelter.

On June 28th we were told that thousands of soldiers were landing at Millbay Docks. We knew from the radio that our army in France was in serious trouble, so we thought they were from Dunkirk but it turned out they were survivors from a troopship the Germans had sunk. Outside the French port of St Nazare, the ship was the ex-liner Lancastria. The captain of the ship had gone to a part of the French coast which was well away from Dunkirk and he was supposed to sail after three days loading men, but he stayed longer to take on more troops. No one knows how many men were on board when she finally sailed, but some say five to six thousand men of which approximately four thousand died. She was spotted by a lone German bomber and hit with three bombs and she sank quickly. A host of small boats saved as many as they could but still thousands drowned below deck. The men who were saved were the men we were talking to and joking with. None of them had any headgear, some had no tunics, some even had no boots, but to us, they were all heroes. I was wearing an artillery badge on my jumper and one of them offered me a pile of French money for it so I gave it to him. The money was worthless of course because the Germans were taking over France.

The odd German air raid carried on during 1940, but still on a small scale and we were beginning to take them in our stride. For a boy my age, it was exciting to roam around my area the morning after a raid. Looking for burnt-out incendiary bombs and shrapnel. I knew how to take an incendiary bomb apart and to keep the tail fin as a souvenir. Shrapnel was a piece of steel from an exploding bomb or shell and there was plenty of it lying around. You could also find pieces of barrage balloon skin and if you were lucky, parachute silk. All the land mines that were dropped came down by parachute.

1941 started quietly for Plymouth and we knew the Battle of Britain was over and hoped it would mean no more raids. We were getting used to rationing, giving coupons for everything…if you could find anything, that is. But it all changed on the night of 20th April 1941 when we had the first raid of the Blitz at Plymouth.

That night it was estimated that over 130 German bombers bombed Plymouth over several hours. We knew it was different by the sound of the plane's engines and by the number of high explosive bombs coming down. These bombs were fitted with whistles, which made a lot of noise as the bomb was falling—our shelter shook several times as large bombs went off, even in the shelter we could hear fire engines, ambulances and the police racing around. When the all-clear sounded and I opened the shelter door, the sky seemed lit up by burning houses. The sky was full of smoke and people were shouting to find out if anyone needed help of any sort. My mother told me to sit on the garden wall and watch Stonehouse Town Hall burning, the flames were high into the sky. What a fire! I knew that I would find plenty of souvenirs the next day.

The following night they came again, over 130 planes starting where they left off the night before. The Blitz lasted seven nights. Several three-story houses in Emma Place were destroyed and one night a neighbour called out to my mother to tell her an incendiary bomb had gone through our roof. She went into the house, up the stairs to her bedroom, and found the bomb lying on her bed. She opened her window and wrapped the top of the bedding around the bomb and shoved it out the window and into the garden. I knew nothing of this because I was in the shelter, but she told me at breakfast the next day. I couldn't get out quick enough—the burnt-out bomb was lying in a pile of ashes. I took the tail fin off for my collection. Sadly, when my mother went to thank the neighbour she found out that he had died of a heart attack after telling her about the bomb.

We had a period of two nights with no raids, then on the 24th of April, it started again and lasted until the 28th of April. The day after the city centre was destroyed my mother took me to see it… what a sight. Acres of rubble still smoking, Marks & Spencer just a pile of iron girders all twisted and bent. Every church burnt out or damaged, it looked like the end for Plymouth.

The next night a land mine hit Emma Place, blowing off the whole front of three large houses. When the land mine exploded our shelter jumped. The next night my mother came and said leave the shelter, sit in your bedroom window (open it first) and watch everything because the Germans were bombing the marine barracks and Millbay Docks.

I sat in the window with my legs hanging over the ledge and it was like being in a war film, only I was in it. The noise was tremendous, with all the ships firing and marines as well—they were using tracer bullets that filled the sky with red, white, green, and yellow streaks. Searchlights were darting around and large anti-aircraft guns were pounding away. On top of all that bombs were going off, fire engines and rescue crews were getting to the scene…it was bedlam. But it was the first raid I had spent watching instead of being in a shelter. That night the Royal Marine Officers' mess was hit and destroyed and a lot of marines died.

The next morning I was on my way to see my pal who lived opposite the marines mess. I saw a marine sentry walking towards me. He said I could not go any further because a large bomb was deep in the road but had not exploded. I asked if I could see it and he let me look. Down a deep hole, I could see the fins of a very large bomb. He told me that the Navy was bringing in a crane to pull it out of the hole and then take it by lorry through the city to the moors, where they would set it off. I went home and told my mother and all she said was, 'I should keep away from Caroline Place 'till it's gone'.

The next night the first two houses in Caroline Place were set on fire. When the all-clear came I got out of the shelter and my mum told me to put my brother to bed and come back out as I was needed to give a hand. Neighbours and firemen were putting furniture and other things from the houses in our lane and I was told to watch over it and to fetch a fireman if anyone tried to take anything. I felt very grown-up that night, doing something so important. The flames from the houses, the smoke and sparks, the firemen shouting to each other and the fact that I was allowed to stay out past midnight…it was a night I will never forget.

More houses in Emma Place were destroyed and Chapel Street was hit badly. The pub my mother worked in was destroyed, as was St Georges Church where she got married. (Despite all this the postman and the milkman continued to turn up day after day delivering the mail and the milk).

The routine after a heavy raid was to get out of the house as early as possible, look for shrapnel and incendiary bombs, then go down and check the school was still standing. Go into the school and in the classroom and check if any desks were empty, if they were we would go out at lunchtime and check out our friends' houses to see if they were okay. There were various reasons for children missing a class. They could be so tired with lack of sleep after a raid that their parents decided to keep them at home. The whole family could have decided to leave Plymouth to live with relations somewhere safe, or they were bombed out so they had to leave anyway.

The worse single event during the Blitz was when a public shelter in Portland Place was hit. When rescue services broke in they found everyone (mainly women and children) sitting on rows of chairs—no wounds, no blood, but all 75 were dead. The exploding bomb blast had sucked the air out of their lungs, killing them instantly.

Chapter 2

I remember 1942 as a good year because the air raids had stopped, except for the only daytime raid I could remember. Our gang of boys was standing at the end of our lane waiting to go down to the school. No siren had gone off and all seemed okay. Then we heard the sound of an aeroplane engine coming up and fast from the naval docks, then a single German fighter zoomed over the marine barracks, firing its guns as it did so—it also fired at ships in Millbay Docks, then it turned back.

The marines were ready then and heavy machine guns opened up from above the barrack entrance. The girls ran screaming to school but the boys ran in the opposite direction towards the barrack entrance because we wanted to collect empty cartridges from the road below the marines' guns. We got our cartridges and were chased away by sentries and we went to school. The Headmaster was waiting. We were lined up and given a real roasting. He told us it was our duty to protect the girls and we should have made certain they all got to school safely. We were never to leave them again…with our pockets full of souvenirs we didn't mind.

We used bomb sites as a playground, every gang had dens, usually cellars or other unsavory places. Health and safety would have had a field day. In 1943, with all fears of a German invasion gone, things started to get more relaxed. We were allowed to go to Devils Point Beach and to use the small swimming pool there. It was here that all the Stonehouse boys learned to swim. We spent all our school holidays at the beach. I would leave home in the morning with sandwiches and a bottle of lemonade and get back in the late afternoon. My mother never worried about me doing this. During our day at the beach, we would get wonderful views of various naval ships coming out of the boatyard. If we saw a single tug come around Devils Point we knew it would be pulling a cruiser, two tugs and it would be a battleship or aircraft carrier. Destroyers and frigates would manage on their own.

The Sunderland flying boats would take off to go and hunt for submarines and if the M.T.B's (Motor Torpedo Boats) were required to rescue any airmen from the English Channel they would roar out past the breakwater at top speed.

We were on a beach but reminded all the time of being at war. There were increasing numbers of American naval and army uniforms in the city, plus stores of tanks, guns, and all types of vehicles including jeeps. All of the American equipment was brand new.

1944 was the time when we were all waiting for the invasion of France, it was also the year I joined the naval cadets, based in the naval barrack Devonport. You had to have a father serving in the navy to be accepted. It was one of the best things I ever did and I had no idea how much it would help me when I joined the army in later years. The cadets taught me how to march, fire a .22 rifle, and look after a uniform.

The ships in Plymouth Sound grew in numbers and there was a lot of activity. We went to look at the ships—they were of all types and sizes but on the morning of 5th June they were all gone. D-Day had started.

In June 1943, my auntie who lived in Scotland offered to put us up for three months so that we could have a break and relax, so off we went by train, my mother, my brother, and myself. My aunt lived in a hamlet called Throsk. It was a place where the security staff that covered a local arms factory lived, everyone was English and all the men where ex-royal marines. Because I was going to be there for three months I had to join the local school which was in the next village, a place called Fallin, not far from the town of Sterling.

I had a shock on my first day to discover that all the other boys in my class came to school wearing just shorts and a singlet. No socks or shoes. They were all miners' children. Fallin had a coal mine and they disliked the English, but after I tried to tell them what the air raids were like and to talk about naval ships, they began to be friendly. One morning I decided to go to school just like them. I removed my shoes and socks and walked into the classroom as if it was the normal thing for me. They were taken completely by surprise, then a couple of them started to laugh and from then on I was accepted. I hid my shoes and socks in a cornfield.

The only history they talked about was a man called Robert the Bruce and another called William Wallace. They knew nothing about English history. I was glad when the three months were up and we were on our way home. I had missed Plymouth and all my pals.

One day in August 1944 my pal David and I decided to go to one of our favourite places to try to catch wild pigeons, we thought we could tame them. Our favourite spot was on the grounds of St George's church and the graveyard around it. The church had been completely ruined in the blitz and the whole site had been sealed off, but we found a way to get in. We had been using it as a play area for ages, no one ever came near it.

We decided to climb a wall that was about ten feet high, the top was covered in ivy. Just as we reached the top and were both getting into the thick ivy, we heard a commotion. A young man of nineteen to twenty years old came into the graveyard the same way we had. Once in, he ran across the graves towards Chapel Street. He was quickly followed by a policeman, both were running really fast. David and I kept still and quiet, giving everything time to settle down. Whilst waiting, I decided to look and see what was on the other side of the wall.

I got a real shock when I did. There was a sheer drop of about forty feet on the other side. It looked like an old quarry because the other two sides going away from the wall were also sheer and it was obviously man-made. Looking at the beginning of the quarry it was open and we could see the water from Stonehouse creek flowing past, the inside of the quarry was overgrown with small bushes and vegetation. Steps had been cut into the right-hand side all the way to the bottom, no handrail, just bare steps. Level with the landing at the left of the steps was a small door set into the wall we were on. We moved along the top of the wall and climbed down behind the door and we were in the quarry. There were so many steps to get to ground level it took us a while. Once we were down we noticed another door set into the base of the sheer cliff that our wall was built on. It was securely closed, obviously, no one was supposed to get in.

At first, we could not understand why anyone would put a door in a cliff face, then we slowly realised we had found the entrance to the caverns under Stonehouse. Most people who had lived in Stonehouse a long time would talk about the caverns, but although we asked everyone, no one could remember where the entrance was. Well, we had found it, no clues from anyone else and nothing to go on, but by a fluke or stroke of luck, we were standing outside the entrance.

We agreed to keep it a secret—we would tell no one. Partly because if our parents knew what we had to do to get into the quarry it would have been out of bounds to us. Also because we did not want others coming down into the quarry as it was our secret. I was ten and so was David when we discovered it. When I spoke to my daughters about it for the very first time years later, I was well into my thirties.

Chapter 3

I think 1945 was a big year for me. First, at the age of 11, I left St Georges School and joined St Peters. I had good news that my father would soon be back with the family…Brilliant! The war finished and Plymouth city started street parties and put on a victory parade. I marched in that parade in my naval uniform, we were determined to show the Royal Marine Cadets how to march. Once the adult section of navy, marines, and army had marched it was our turn. I remember coming down North Hill, I was in the front row because I was tall. As we got to the saluting base a naval band struck up '*Hearts of Oak*' and what a difference it made to us. We marched better than we had ever done before. It was a great experience. My father came back towards to end of the year and that was great.

1946 was a good year. My father was bending over backwards to make up for lost time and he took me everywhere with him at every opportunity. His first job was driving a naval ambulance. I lost count of the number of times I went into the naval barracks sat in the back of an ambulance. He then drove the commander's car for a while and would take me for a drive whenever he was not on duty. His final role was as a driver for Plymouth naval shore patrols. He drove a vehicle, which had a box at the back for prisoners, and my dad drove with a patrolman in front and a patrolman behind him, all out in the open. I saw them on patrol several times in Union Street and I would wave and the whole patrol would wave back.

Unfortunately in 1947, my father was admitted to the naval hospital in Stonehouse. He was suffering from TB from which there was no cure in those days. I would go with my mother to visit him three nights a week for several hours to try and cheer him up but he was slowly fading away. The day I came home from school to be told he had died was not a surprise. I remember the funeral. After the church service, we walked towards the grave and my mother said, 'Stand by my side, take my hand, and don't let go.' I could tell she was shaking. As the coffin was put into the grave a squad of sailors with rifles fired a salute and it was over.

One evening after we were being dismissed from being on parade in our naval cadet uniforms an officer gave us a surprise. He said if anyone wanted to stay behind they would be allowed to go on board the latest battleship in the Royal Navy, H.M.S. Vanguard. About twelve of us decided to give it a go. We were taken by lorry to the naval dockyard. H.M.S. Vanguard was in dry dock. We roamed all over the ship, it was lovely, the battleship was huge, and to me, it looked unsinkable. I climbed up to touch the gold crown on the top of the short flag pole at the bow. Now anytime I see a picture of Vanguard it all comes back to me.

In 1948, money was tight at home so I got myself a job as a paperboy, doing a paper round before going to school and another round after school. The money was not much but it helped my mother. I met a friend who was wearing an RAF uniform. He told me he had joined the air training corps so that he could fly in RAF Dakotas. I thought about it and decided to resign from the naval cadets and join the air training corps. Within a couple of months, I got my first chance.

I was told to be at Roborough airfield on a Thursday afternoon to be met by the airman who would be flying us in a Dakota aeroplane. It was great, we flew out to the Eddystone Lighthouse, back to the coast and past all the southwest resorts, and then back to Roborough. It was a fantastic experience, but the next day in school I was called out at assembly to give the school a talk on what it was like to fly. At that moment I was the only pupil who had ever done it.

1949 was the year I would leave school at fifteen to start work. I started to approach various companies asking for an apprenticeship. I finally got one with a firm of architectural engineers called Woodrow Metals. My apprenticeship would be from 1949 - 1954 when I would be 20 years old, so I packed in my paper round that Saturday and started on Monday.

In March 1949 my brother Gordon reached the age of fifteen and surprised us all by enlisting in the army as a boy soldier serving in the artillery.

Chapter 4

From 1949 to 1953 the job went really well. I found no problem in reading engineers' drawings, welding, oxy burning, and all the things that were required of me.

In 1952 I met the girl I would marry, Margaret Stanaway-Ivey. She was 17 years old. Towards the end of my apprenticeship (July 1954) I had to decide if I wanted to do two years of national service or sign up as a three-year short term regular. I would only be able to pick my regiment if I was a regular, so I decided to sign up for three years in the Royal Military Police.

Just days before my 20th birthday I was ordered to go to Inkerman Barracks, Woking, for 12 weeks training. I was the first recruit to arrive and was shown to a large barrack room and told to select a bed. The next recruit to walk into the room was a Geordie lad called Frank Nee who would become my best friend in the army.

By day three there were about twelve of us doing nothing when a sergeant came and told us he would be our drill sergeant and there would finally be thirty-five of us in Sp Dup 439. His job was to teach us to march and everything else to make us fit to be Redcaps. By the end of the week, the sergeant asked to see me. He said he would be appointing a recruit to be his right-hand man. This person would be required to march the squad and parade around and also be responsible for ensuring the barrack room was kept tidy at all times. He knew I had been in two types of cadets and considered I was just the person for the job.

I accepted at once. I wasn't bothered about drilling the squad, someone had to do it. I had an interview with the Commanding Officer who agreed I should be given the role, so I was promoted to Squad Lance Corporal and told to get my stripes on asap.

So in less than two weeks, I had a stripe and a rank. I had no problems from the squad and I don't think anyone else fancied doing it anyway.

Training went well and we were getting near to the end which would be a passing out parade (at which point all the squad would be wearing a stripe). The sergeant knew Frank was a good friend of mine and asked to see us both a day before the parade. He had a complete list of all the postings the squad would fill and as a thank you for my help he let us pick our posting. We chose Fontainebleau, in France. He told us not to say a word to anyone and to look surprised when the list was put on daily orders.

The passing out parade went well and we were all sent on two weeks' leave.

I went home to Plymouth to get married on 16th October 1954. After a honeymoon in London, I was on my way to France for nine months.

We were billeted in Quartier Chateau, a large building inside four high walls, the security was provided by Redcaps, twenty-four seven. The duties were easy and it proved to be a cushy number. The most memorable thing to happen was being told to attend a function that Field Marshal Montgomery would be attending. He sent a message saying he wanted the NCO's (Non-commissioned Officers) who took part to be smarter than the American police who would also be attending. Frank and I spent half a day getting buffed up, we made certain that Field Marshal Montgomery would not be able to complain.

Everything was going well. I was on duty stopping French traffic at the main road junction, Frank was at the venue entrance. We both had to salute as the field marshal's car passed us (the car was flying a flag and had a board showing he was a field marshal) and I could feel the field marshal's eyes on me. I walked back to meet Frank and we stood close to where Montgomery was standing, talking to American officers. Suddenly he turned around and before we could jump to attention he just said, 'Well done, boys.'

We were just standing around wondering how long we had to wait when an American officer walked towards us. He had a bottle in each hand. He came up and said, 'Compliments of the Field Marshal', and held out a bottle of champagne and a bottle of whisky. We were speechless. To be given a gift from the highest-ranking man in the British army was an honour as far as we were concerned… the man was a legend.

Shortly afterwards, on 17th July 1955, we got orders to report to London District Church Street, Kensington Palace Barracks. On the channel ferry, I told Frank it was my 21st birthday. 'Come on, I'll treat you to a drink,' he said.

Not one birthday card, no mobile phone to speak to Margaret or anyone, it was a 21st birthday I would remember for all the wrong reasons.

Our duties in London were completely different from anything we had done so far. Our first four duties were to go to various RAF bases to meet planes bringing army prisoners back from Germany. If a man was sentenced to five years he would have to serve it in a civil prison in London. During our journey across London, the prisoner had to be handcuffed to one of us at all times—it made people get out of the way once they saw the handcuffs.

We had to take one prisoner to Colchester Military Prison, we went by train in a reserved compartment. When we arrived at the prison and went through the gates little did I know that years later my brother, who had transferred to the military police and reached the rank of R.S.M., would have the job of running this prison.

We also did foot patrols from Piccadilly Circus to Soho and Trafalgar Square. I then became a dispatch rider on a new Triumph 500cc motorbike which I enjoyed immensely.

Chapter 5

One day, a notice on the duty board stated that members from London would be sent to Cyprus to help restore law and order from terrorists. Only men with one and a half years' service would be sent. Frank was a national serviceman who only had six months to serve so for us it was the parting of the ways. We were sent home on a 48-hour pass, then we went back to Inkerman barracks for a week's training on firing our .38 revolvers and Sten guns. We would be in Cyprus for one and a half years.

The RAF flew us to Malta, then on to Nicosia, Cyprus. We landed late at night and were told to just lie down inside some tents, no beds, our kit bags were our pillows.

The next morning we lined up to be told who was going where. An officer walked down the line and then put out his hand and said everyone at this point will be staying in Nicosia. He put out his hand again and said everyone from here (which included me) would be going to Limassol. Everyone else would go to Larnaca. Twelve of us would be the new section with two land rovers.

All we knew at that point was that we were going to a place called Gibraltar camp. As we got to Limassol and turned into the road leading to the camp, we saw a large sign which read Gibraltar camp 3rd Commando Brigade.

I could not have been more pleased because I knew that all marines passed through the Stonehouse barracks in those days and we would have a lot to talk about. At first, the marines, who were a lot older than us, called us the *Schoolboy Policemen* but when they saw what we did they eventually had a lot of respect for us and treated us very well.

After picking which tents to have and unpacking our gear, we got down to deciding what to do first. It was decided to start doing foot patrols of Limassol to let the locals know that we were going to restore law and order. An NCO called Jim Vickers and myself would do the first patrol next morning and two others would take over the afternoon patrol. The first day went well with no trouble but the next day was somewhat different.

As Jim and I walked along the main road one of our land rovers came along at speed, telling us we had to go back to camp a.s.a.p. It turned out that the second-in-command at Nicosia had been shot and killed while out on foot patrol and an NCO had been injured. From now on all foot patrols were cancelled, which gave Jim and myself a record as we had carried out the first foot patrol of Limassol and also the last.

It was decided that all future patrols would be mobile ones, a land rover with three men—a driver, front escort, and rear escort. We were told to remove the roof from the land rover, take the top off the doors and have the vehicles open all round. We then put a layer of filled sandbags on the floor at the back. The REME (Royal Electrical and Mechanical

Engineers) welded a wire cutter to the front bumper and then we were ready to start patrol.

The land rovers did not have a radio, so once we left the camp no one would have any idea where we were. We could not call for help or ask for advice, once we were on patrol we would be on our own. One NCO would be in charge. He would make the decisions and the other two would back him to the hilt. The average age of a patrolman was 19 years old.

The procedure for going on patrol would be. Get dressed, take your .38 revolver outside the tent and fill it with six bullets. Put it in your holster, then go to the armoury and sign out an automatic gun (mine was a tommy gun). Get two magazines of ammunition, one tear gas grenade, and then you were ready. Our .38 Smith and Wesson revolvers were all stamped with *property of N.Y. police department.* It turned out that after Dunkirk the British army was so short of weapons that the New York police voted to send all their small arms to the British military police.

Your revolver stayed with you at all times and when you finished patrol you took out the bullets and put the gun and ammo in your tent. We only had empty orange boxes to store things in. The tents could not be locked, so to give us security our MP tents were strictly out of bounds to all marines regardless of rank. It is worth a few words on who we were fighting.

It was a terrorist group called EOKA (a Greek Cypriot nationalist guerrilla organisation who was fighting for the end of British rule in Cyprus). They were led by an ex-colonel in the Greek army called Colonel Grivas. He arrived in Cyprus in 1955 and recruited men from villages in the Troodos mountain area as well as from Nicosia, Limassol, Larnaca, and Famagusta.

They started killing members of the Turkish police in 1955. They started on the British military in 1956. We were told we would be dealing with the local population as well as the military. The Greeks hated the Turkish police who felt the same about the Greeks. Both sides mistrusted us and we mistrusted them in turn. Life was not easy in Cyprus in the '50s. During the EOKA campaign, the number of servicemen who were killed was 371. At the same time, about 1,000 civilians also died.

It took us a while to find our way around Limassol. We covered every lane, street, and road. The most difficult area was known as the Casbah—it was the oldest part of the town with very narrow streets. It was the Casbah area that gave us our first taste of what a strange place Limassol was.

We were on patrol when we heard a bang. We headed to the area which was in a street in the Casbah. When we got there the whole street was empty of civilians. All we could see was a cart with a donkey stuck in the shafts. The donkey had a large hole in his chest with blood pouring out, but every door was closed and all the windows too—nobody wanted to be involved. We considered that it could have been an explosive device that went off by mistake, hitting the donkey, but whatever it was we were not going to find out, so we decided to drive off and return later.

From Boyhood To Redcap

When we returned the street was empty...no cart, no donkey. All the blood washed away, still not a person in sight. We knew our time there would not be dull. The following week we were involved in dealing with our first riot.

We were heading for Heroes Square when we saw a large crowd coming down the road towards us. The men had sticks, the women did not carry anything but they were all making as much noise as possible. We had not been given any training on riot control. We had no riot shields or anything like that, so we stopped and waited for them to get really close, and then we threw a couple of our tear gas grenades and the crowd started to break up. In fact, they started running away. We reported the incident and asked for advice on how to deal with future riots but we were told to do the same as we had already done. Typical British army!

Chapter 6

One thing the army did do was to send up a spotter plane to stop riots starting. The army air corps sent a small single-engine plane to Limassol and it used a nearby field to land in. It was decided that a Redcap would go with the plane to fly around Limassol looking for any crowds of people. The pilot would then radio the location and our patrols would break them up. Because my records showed I had been in the air training corps it was decided I would go up in the plane. It was great. It only lasted a couple of days because the locals soon realised what was going on but I enjoyed the experience.

We then found out that a mobile patrol of Redcaps had been attacked in Nicosia with one NCO killed and one wounded. Dangerous times indeed.

We were informed that four NCO's would be required to attend a function at a camp called Episkopi, it was one of the largest camps on the island, but we had to be wearing our military police No. 1 dress uniforms. Well, only three of us had been issued with them, so the sergeant said he would go with us.

We were told we would be leaving at four o'clock the next day. We were also told we would not be taking any weapons but we would be protected by the driver and one escort. This was because the dress uniform did not allow for a weapon to be carried.

All three of us protested that this was not right, remembering what had happened to the patrol of Redcaps, but the sergeant overruled us and so we left for Episkopi and arrived with no problems.

The function went well and we were dismissed at 10.30 pm. We were due to meet our land rover to return at 11.00 pm. It would be parked and waiting at the camp entrance.

I started to wander towards the entrance—I was alone and had no idea where the rest of our party was. As I got closer the sergeant of the guard came out and started to run towards me. I knew at once that something was wrong. He told me that our land rover had been ambushed on the Kourion Heights on the way in and that both Redcaps had been wounded. I asked where they were and he said at the medical centre. I told him to take me there at once.

When I got to the centre a medic told me that the driver had gunshot wounds to his legs but the escort was badly wounded. The driver was being tended to by doctors in another building but the escort was lying on a stretcher. I sat beside him and at first, I could not see that he had been shot. He was deeply unconscious and I could not see any wound until I looked behind his right ear. There was an entry wound at the base of his skull but the bullet was still in his head.

His name was Albert Shaw and he was nineteen years old. I asked a medic what was going to happen to Albert and he told me that surgeons at RAF Akrotiri were waiting for him and they would operate straight away. The trouble was, Albert was just lying there, and as far as I could see nobody was doing anything to get him to Akrotiri.

When I asked why he was not on his way the answer was hard to believe. I was told an ambulance was ready but it needed an armed escort before it could leave. I asked where Albert's gun was and they showed me and I picked it up and said right, I will be the escort, get Albert in the ambulance now. I looked for our sergeant but he was still missing as were the other two Redcaps. I did not really have the authority to appoint myself as the escort or to give orders to the medical staff but they obeyed anyway. I had come so far, there was no turning back.

I got in the ambulance and spoke to the driver while Albert was being placed inside. An army padre asked if he could ride in the back, I said okay and we set off. The entrance to the camp was open and we drove through and then we were on our own.

I asked the driver if he knew the way to Akrotiri—his answer surprised me. He said that this was the first time he had been out of camp during darkness (it was now well past 11 o'clock). The custom at the camp was for everyone to be in before it was dark, then the camp was locked up. I explained that we were out on patrol every night and it was nothing to worry about and I would tell him the way to Akrotiri. The ambulance was climbing up the Kourion Heights and I was picturing the road ahead because I knew that near the top was where the ambush had taken place. We were very close to the spot when there was the sound of someone hammering on the ambulance partition. I told the driver to stop and go back and find out what the padre wanted. The lights were switched off and I got out and climbed up the embankment to get to the grassy top. I needed to be able to see anyone coming onto the road and coming across to the grassy area. It was warm, there was no wind and the only light was from a half-moon. There was also total silence. It was very lonely standing up in no man's land and it seemed an age before I heard the driver shout to me.

I got down into the ambulance and the driver told me the padre had thought that Albert was gone, but he found a faint pulse so we still had a chance of getting him to Akrotiri alive. We reached the top of the heights, a place known as Apollo's Temple, and I knew we had passed the ambush spot and it was all downhill from now. We got onto the Akrotiri road and as we approached the large RAF base we could see that members of the RAF Regiment were waiting at the entrance and were waving us on. We went in and stopped. As I got out an RAF member climbed in and said he would direct the driver straight to the operating theatre. I had done all I could to give Albert a chance. I had got him to Akrotiri alive.

I spent the night in a chair in the guard room, but in the early hours, I was told that Albert had died during the operation. It was a bad end to a bad night. A patrol picked me up and took me back to Gibraltar camp. I went to the police tent and noticed two sergeants I had not seen before. They asked if I was okay then said they were from Head Quarters sent to help clear things up. Nobody asked how I came to be at Akrotiri, or what had happened at Episkopi. I was not asked to write a report so I left.

Three days later Albert Shaw's funeral was organised and I was asked if I wanted to be a pallbearer. I said yes. On the day six of us left for Waynes Keep, Nicosia. This was the military cemetery guarded by Redcaps who also ran the military prison. We carried Albert's coffin to the grave. A padre gave a small sermon, there was no gun salute. The coffin was put in the grave, we saluted and that was it. Not one member of Albert's family were present, they would not have been able to get to Cyprus in time, and he only had six of his friends to see him on his way. It was very sad.

We got back to Limassol and tried to put it behind us. Then I was given a completely different job. I was instructed to pick a driver whom I considered good enough to get me to a small landing strip in the Troodos Mountains. From there I would pick up a major in the royal marines and deliver him safely to Gibraltar camp. I only trusted one driver called Willie, he had been the driver on nearly all my patrols, plus he and I had been to the airstrip before. When I told him he was all for it.

To ensure we were at the airstrip by 0800 am we had to leave the camp at 5.30 am. The journey up went well. We bypassed every village to avoid anyone from EOKA seeing us. We took a track to go the rest of the way as the main road was always being spied on. The small army air corps plane landed dead on time and our Major got out and walked towards us. We should have known that a major in the marines would be smart, well, he was immaculate. Willie and myself, plus the land rover, were covered in dust due to our driving on the rough track. We saluted him and held the door open for him. He did not look happy. He said he had been expecting to be met by marine commandos, not Redcaps. We told him that no marine drivers had ever driven up the Troodos mountains so we had been given the job. We gave him a Sten gun and said we thought he would be happier if he had a weapon, just in case.

He asked questions all the way back to the camp, about Limassol, about our patrols, about the local people, everything. We got back in good time and delivered a very dusty major to the waiting marines. He thanked us and said he felt he was in safe hands. A job well done.

Our old sergeant was put on a charge by the CO. He was found guilty of neglect of duty in sending us out unarmed. He was reduced to Lance Corporal and posted to the U.K. We were told a new one was on his way from Germany and would arrive in days. We then received bad news. Two of the lads who came out with us and went to Larnaca had been killed—they were off duty inside a walled garden and enjoying a drink when EOKA threw a bomb over the wall and they died instantly.

Our new sergeant arrived and he looked really smart, a true military policeman. But he only came out on patrol twice and that was in daylight. He said he thought he was better employed staying in the police office where H.Q. Nicosia could contact him anytime. We didn't mind at all as we had been doing patrols on our own for ages anyway.

From Boyhood To Redcap

The army top brass in Nicosia had planned an exercise that would involve putting hundreds of troops into the Troodos Mountains to drive out members of EOKA, but after the troops had got so far into the forest, EOKA started several forest fires. Groups of men were trapped and could not find a way out…it was a disaster.

At the end of the day 14 members of the Gordon Highlanders were dead, 5 men of the Green Howards and 2 men of the Parachute Regiment. EOKA had come out on top. We blamed the top brass for putting men into the mountains who had never been there before. To lose 21 men was a very high price to pay.

Several days later we were informed that two, five-ton lorries would arrive at Gibraltar camp. We were told that two Redcaps were to show them where to park (away from any other vehicles) and to stop anyone from getting near them. Another two Redcaps would escort the drivers to the cookhouse for a meal and ensure no one spoke to them. We could not understand why we were being told to keep the drivers and escorts away from everyone else in the camp.

When the two lorries arrived we instantly knew why. The lorries had the bodies of the Gordon Highlanders inside and they smelt absolutely awful. The smell was part wood fire and something else that was like nothing we had ever smelt before. We knew the lorries were being used to take the bodies of the 14 men who had died in the Troodos fires back to the camp of the Gordons at Nicosia. We were glad to see them leave. We felt sorry for them but there was nothing we could do to make it easier for them.

From Boyhood To Redcap

We were on patrol in Limassol a couple of days later and noticed a new shop had opened. We had a word with the owner because we were not sure what he was selling. It turned out he was offering to supply air tickets and hotel bookings to anyone flying out of Nicosia airport. I asked him how much a return ticket to Heathrow London would cost and he said £40 which seemed a good price. Several days later, after thinking about it, I told several of the lads that I was going to ask for two weeks' leave. They fell about laughing because no one had ever gone home on leave from Gibraltar camp before, or Cyprus itself really. I asked our sergeant to put in an application to H.Q. for me. He also said you are wasting your time, it will never be granted. To everyone's surprise a week later H.Q. gave me the green light to go ahead.

I bought a ticket the next day. When the day for the flight arrived a patrol took me to Nicosia airport and I flew to Rome and then to London. I had been given a travel warrant to go by train to Plymouth (return) and I had two lovely weeks with Margaret. The return trip went well and the lads were waiting to take me back to Limassol.

The first thing the boys told me was that all future applications for leave would be turned down. The top brass had decided that if men started going on leave willy-nilly it would create chaos. I think my application took them by surprise. They said yes because they were wrong-footed but soon realised that they had to stop it as soon as possible.

We heard on the grapevine that Britain and France were going to invade Egypt to free up the Suez Canal which had been taken over by the Egyptians. The marines were convinced they would be going, as did other units, but even though 20,000 troops were on Cyprus the army began to send men from the U.K. for the invasion.

British and French paratroops started to arrive and also the infantry. We were surprised that thousands of reservists were arriving as well. The commandos were really upset about not going, it would have given them something to do.

We were kept really busy directing men and equipment to various sites. Days before the invasion men were sent to Limassol for loading on to various naval vessels because Limassol docks had good facilities for loading ships. The sea around Limassol had a large number of ships just waiting, then, just like D-Day, one morning they were all gone. We heard the invasion went really well and the Egyptians were soon pushed back and the Suez Canal was opened again. However, America did not agree with what we and the French had done and our men were taken out of Egypt and returned to the U.K.

Chapter 7

It was getting near to Christmas and the marines invited 20 crew members of a naval destroyer to spend an evening in our canteen talking and drinking beer (the beer would be free). They asked us to have a patrol to escort the coach arriving from the docks to Gibraltar camp.

The sailors arrived at our camp at about 6 pm. We were asked to escort them back to the docks by 10.30 pm but the patrol who escorted them in told us there was a big problem. It turned out that to go into or out of the docks required passing through a square around which new shops and houses were being built. They said it was the perfect ambush spot, with a lot of empty windows overlooking the square which EOKA could use. We all got together in our tents to work out a plan to protect the navy and protect ourselves. It took a lot of talking before we decided what we would do.

Instead of one patrol, we would use two. When the first patrol reached the square they would put on speed, do a U-turn and jump out of the land rover and find three separate places to hide. The coach driver would be told to just keep driving into the docks. The second patrol would then be at the square and if they heard shooting they would stop, get out and approach the square from a different way. We reckoned that six heavily armed Redcaps would have been able to pack a fair punch and that EOKA would not fancy taking us on. If nothing happened that was a bonus, we would still have been able to practice something that we could always use another day. In fact, it all turned out well.

One day we were on patrol in Limassol and it had been quite a morning because we had made arrangements to meet the other patrol at the main police station to have lunch in the Turkish canteen. We were now heading in the direction of the police station. Suddenly we heard a burst of gunfire and we knew from the sound it was from a Sten gun. Putting on speed we arrived to see the other patrol parked outside the station. The three members of the patrol were talking to two British infantry soldiers, there were also several groups of Turkish police talking together as well. An NCO called Ginger came up to us saying he was in big trouble and explained that as he jumped out of the land rover somehow his Sten gun was activated, his finger was on the trigger and it started firing. By the time he took his finger off the trigger, he had shot some holes down the side of a five-ton army lorry belonging to an infantry unit. Also, when the Sten gun started firing, a Turkish policeman who was guarding the entrance to the police station inside a sandbag pillbox fainted...he thought he was under attack.

We knew we had to sort it out to save Ginger from being put on a charge. I spoke to the Turkish super who said he wasn't bothered by an army lorry getting holes in it and the Turkish policeman was the laughing stock of the station for fainting, so as far as he was concerned nothing happened. That was the first hurdle over. We told the two infantry boys we would follow them to their unit where we would talk to the sergeant in charge of transport, which we did. Luckily he saw the funny side of the situation and said if we could get REME to repair the holes he would cover up for us. The REME unit owed us a favour so all ended well, but Ginger will never forget it.

Christmas 1956 went well. The marines laid on a great spread which was served to us at breakfast and dinner by the marine officers. The only fly in the ointment was that we were told to continue patrols every day during Christmas because otherwise, EOKA would take advantage. I should have mentioned earlier that the Greek Orthodox Church was supporting EOKA therefore every priest and church were suspect, but we were forbidden to enter any church due to the top brass thinking it would turn every Greek against us. The head of the Greek Church was Archbishop Makarios. The British government had him kidnapped and put on an RAF plane and flown out of Cyprus and into exile. You can imagine how pleased the Greeks were about that.

1957 started well and I was promoted to full corporal and given my second stripe. We were told we were going to do a different sort of patrol which would be known as a Q patrol. We would patrol in unmarked civilian cars, we would be in civilian clothes and we were issued with special shoulder holsters so that when we put on windcheaters no one would see we were armed. It worked for a couple of days, then we realised the locals knew what was happening, they were even waving to us as we went by.

Whoever had planned Q patrols had forgotten that the Greeks who lived in Limassol were born and bred there. They would spot a strange car being driven by young men who did not look Greek, so that was the end of the Q patrols, which was a pity but we enjoyed it while it lasted.

One morning we were on patrol early in one of Limassol's many roads when we saw an RAF car about 50 feet away, parked with the hood up, and an air force member leaning over the engine. He had no idea what was going on behind him, he was a prime target. We were moving slowly due to the rush hour traffic and locals darting across the road. We saw a Greek man walk out of a side street, he walked quickly across the road and approached the car behind the airman. In full view of the patrol, he pulled out a revolver and shot the airman once in the back. He then melted away into the crowd. We could not fire because of the number of people in front of us. We got out of the land rover and got to him as soon as we could. He was still bending over the engine. We lifted him up and he started talking to us and we thought he was okay. We could see he had been shot through the left shoulder. Shock soon set him off shaking, so we put him in our patrol car and took him to the main police station in Limassol. We got on the phone to Akrotiri who said an ambulance was on its way. It was not a good way to start the day, however, he lived to tell the tale.

We were on patrol one afternoon, it had been quiet up until then, and we reached the end of the beach road where the road to Nicosia started. We were turning when we saw the owner of a taverna on the Nicosia road waving to us. When we reached him he said there was a track just past the taverna which led to the sea—he said we should go down it because there was something he thought we should see but he did not want to be involved. He did not want to be mentioned in any report. We drove down the track until we reached an army champ, parked at the end (a champ is an upgraded land rover only issued to specific units).

In the back of the champ were two sterling submachine guns, fully loaded, and two complete sets of army uniforms. We could tell from the jackets that they belonged to officers of the Blues and Royals which were also known as the Household Cavalry. The officers' ranks were known as ensigns. We unloaded the weapons and put them in our land rover for safety and we then went looking for the officers. We found them lying on the beach in just their underwear, both out for the count. We tried waking them, without success. We tried shouting but got no response…they were as drunk as it was possible to be. It was obvious they had been drinking heavily, gone for a swim, then laid out in the sun and passed out. To do that in Cyprus was just asking for trouble.

They couldn't walk so we had to carry them, one at a time and lay them in the back of our land rover. We just threw their uniforms on top of them. We decided to take them back to the Blues and Royals camp which was about three miles from Gibraltar camp. When we arrived at the entrance of the camp I told the guard we wanted someone to fetch the RSM as quickly as possible. I told the guard commander not to let anyone from the camp go near us. Even he was not to get close until his RSM was present. When the RSM arrived he did not look pleased, he didn't like to be asked to go to the camp entrance by Redcaps, however, when we showed him what was in our land rover he went ballistic, shouting for the guards, giving orders to everyone and really acting just like we knew he would. When the officers had been taken away we handed over the two weapons and gave him the full story. I explained that we had not placed them under arrest because they would not have understood it so I asked him if he would take them over and for the regiment to deal with them themselves. While talking to us he became really friendly, he said the Blues and Royals owed us and thanked us for bringing them back and not letting the other units see them. I told him I would be back the next day with a report giving all the relevant facts for the C.O.

The next morning I gave him my report and once again he said if there was anything the Blues and Royals could do to help us we only had to ask. I asked if there was any way I could get hold of one of their revolver holders, they were far better than ours. He said if I called into their guardroom the next day I would find a package waiting for me.

I got my holster. It was a pity the two officers had let the Blues and Royals down because during the EOKA campaign several men of the regiment were killed.

Chapter 8

We were beginning to think that perhaps EOKA were relaxing their activities, they were very quiet and fewer reports were coming in about servicemen being attacked. We were on patrol one night knowing that due to the local curfew being eased, the open-air cinema would be open. This had been closed for some time. The cinema was just four walls with one entrance and a large screen at one end. It did not have a roof.

As the evening got later we decided to drive around the cinema just to check it out. We had driven around three of the walls and all seemed okay, but as we were approaching the end of the last wall, out of the corner of my eye I saw an object come over the wall towards us. I shouted *bomb* (which was our normal warning) and the driver stuck his foot down, but there was no explosion. We did another circuit until we were back where we had started. We turned the headlights on full and started searching. About four feet from where the side of our land rover had been we found a hand grenade. The pin was out, so it should have gone off, but thank god it didn't because we would all have been hit by shrapnel if it had.

We knew it would have been a waste of time stopping anyone leaving the cinema because they were all Greek

Cypriots who would only say they knew nothing about it anyway. We had to send for the bomb disposal crew to take it away. It was very unstable so they put sandbags around it and set it off where it lay. We considered it to be a very lucky night for us…very lucky indeed.

Shortly after this, I was asked if I would take on the responsibility of covering all traffic accidents involving military vehicles within a 10-mile radius of Limassol town centre. It would also involve being the first Redcap to respond to any reports of military personnel being AWOL (absent without leave). I didn't think I would get any of those due to all units being confined to camp. I was given a driver who would only work for me with a dedicated land rover. I did not have to report to anyone. I would be completely on my own. It was too good to turn down and I started right away.

My driver was called Ginger and we got on really well together. Once I was given details of an accident I would get to the location and start work. The first thing to do was to see if anyone was badly hurt, then I would ensure that they were taken care of—Military personnel to Akrotiri and civilians to Limassol hospital. I would then pick a good focal point and take dimensions of all points on the vehicles involved so that I could produce a plan showing the position of the vehicles at the time of the accident and take a statement from each driver, plus any other witnesses. Once the vehicles had been removed I would return to camp and notify any army units whose vehicles were involved, giving a quick outlook on who would possibly be at fault. I would prepare a plan and write a report on the accident. If it was military only I would take one copy of my report and all statements and hand it to the sergeants in charge of transport in both units involved. In my report, I would offer to attend any enquiry the unit may decide to hold. Then, unless I was asked, my job was finished.

But if civilian vehicles were involved then I would take a copy of everything to the main Turkish police station in Limassol and offer to attend court if required. So from attending the accident to calling at various camps/police station it was a full-time job. Most accidents were minor and did not produce any real problems but we had a report of a five-ton army lorry abandoned on the Limassol to Troodos road. When we arrived we checked inside the back—it was completely empty, no driver or escort. We then noticed that the front passenger door window was shattered, the glass being inside the cab. I opened the driver's door and saw the vehicle documents lying on the seat, they were covered in something which I started to clean off until I realised it was brains.

We decided to return to camp and then to phone around to find out which unit it belonged to, but when we got back the unit had already reported to us. It seems there were two lorries, and a bomb went off beside the first one. The second lorry stopped, they put the first lorry driver in their lorry and drove him to Akrotiri to get medical help, but he was dead on arrival.

Attending accidents became routine but it was a job I really enjoyed. Then the day arrived when I had to carry out the other part of my job, tracking down AWOL personnel. Just as we were going out one morning a royal marine officer reported that three Marines were AWOL. He gave us full details of each one, said they were not armed, and he was worried that they would be very vulnerable. As soon as we saw their names we knew exactly who they were. We told him we would start searching right away.

Our first port of call was the main brothel behind the police station. Sure enough, they were inside. They were told to dress, they were then arrested and taken back to camp. The marine officer was still in our police tent when I told him I wanted to hand three prisoners over to him—he could hardly believe it, it had taken us forty-five minutes from start to finish. The marines were really impressed (although not the three who were arrested).

It was getting very close to the time when we would be going back to the UK to be demobbed. The Greek Cypriot who was responsible for collecting all the washing for our police section asked me and Ginger if we would have an evening meal at his house, his mother very much wanted us to come. We asked where he lived and when he said Berengaria, we knew we had a problem.

That particular village was out of bounds to everyone, it was considered so pro EOKA that drivers were told not to drive through it. When we told him this he laughed and said the village had voted communist at the last elections. He said we would be safer there than anywhere else. He even said the village elders would have our land rover guarded all the time we were in the village so we said okay and accepted his invitation.

From Boyhood To Redcap

When the evening arrived we drove to Berengaria. He was waiting outside his house with several other men who had been told to guard our vehicle. We had a good meal with his parents, it was a pie with vegetables. We asked what the small meaty lumps were and he said, 'Sparrow.' The practice in Cyprus was to catch small birds and cook them in pies. We still enjoyed the meal and were glad we had decided to go.

But things were starting to change at the camp. The marines were told to get ready to leave Cyprus, they would start leaving in a couple of weeks. I was told to be ready to leave on a troopship with three other Redcaps from Nicosia in three days.

On the way from camp to Limassol docks, it felt a bit strange because I would soon be sailing away. We boarded the troopship and settled into our cabins. When the ship did sail we went out on deck to bid Limassol farewell, because we had no idea if we would ever see it again. The ship was slow but I suppose it was not in a race to get back to the UK. The weather was good and the food on board was very good. At times it was boring but every day was getting us closer to home. We reached Malta and an officer came to see us, he said they wanted to let the lads have six hours ashore but it could only happen if we volunteered to go ashore on duty to do a foot patrol of the main area of bars. The area was known on Malta as Strait Street or the Gut. We had to say yes, so we were the first off the ship. The lads gave us no trouble at all, they were all back by four o'clock. We were the last back, job done.

When we reached our cabins and started to remove our red caps and MP armbands we realised it was for the last time and we would never go on foot patrol again. We would never walk around with loaded weapons again, we would miss the feel of our revolvers on our left hips. Life was going to change.

The ship sailed on past Gibraltar and into the Bay of Biscay. I thought that the next day we would be sailing up the west coast of Cornwall but instead, we had gone around Lands End and were sailing up the north Cornish coast. We sailed all day and night, then we woke and the ship was still and quiet. We went on deck and the first thing we saw was a very large building with two huge statues of birds on each front face (we found out later that we had been looking at the famous Liver Birds). The ship was moored up in Liverpool docks. We travelled by train to London and on to Woking and Inkerman Barracks.

The action of being demobbed took about thirty minutes and once we had handed all our kit in it was over.

I stood on the station platform at Woking waiting for the Plymouth train to arrive. I was really glad to be going home to Margaret. During my last 18 months, I had only been home for two weeks. I was a civilian again and I would be looking for a job.

It was my 23rd birthday and during those 23 years I had experienced many things, some good and some bad, but to be truthful, apart from the death of my father, I would not have changed a thing.

Printed in Great Britain
by Amazon

73585529R00031